Holy Miracles

Incredible True Short Stories
of God's Amazing Miracles

BY EVANGELINA CASAREZ

BALBOA.
PRESS

A DIVISION OF HAY HOUSE

Balboa Press books may be ordered through booksellers or by contacting:

Balboa Press
A Division of Hay House
1663 Liberty Drive
Bloomington, IN 47403
www.balboapress.com
1-(877) 407-4847

Because of the dynamic nature of the Internet, any web addresses or
links contained in this book may have changed since publication and
may no longer be valid. The views expressed in this work are solely those
of the author and do not necessarily reflect the views of the publisher,
and the publisher hereby disclaims any responsibility for them.

The author of this book does not dispense medical advice or prescribe the use
of any technique as a form of treatment for physical, emotional, or medical
problems without the advice of a physician, either directly or indirectly. The
intent of the author is only to offer information of a general nature to help
you in your quest for emotional and spiritual well-being. In the event you use
any of the information in this book for yourself, which is your constitutional
right, the author and the publisher assume no responsibility for your actions.

Any people depicted in stock imagery provided by Thinkstock are
models, and such images are being used for illustrative purposes only.
Certain stock imagery © Thinkstock.

Printed in the United States of America.

ISBN: 978-1-4525-7514-8 (sc)
ISBN: 978-1-4525-7515-5 (e)

Balboa Press rev. date: 7/08/2013

Dedication

With love and gratitude, I dedicate this book to God, our Savior the Lord Jesus Christ, Mother Mary and all the Heavenly Angels who had a part in my miracles. Thank you for your love and guidance.

Acknowledgement

Many thanks to my daughter Samantha Romel for helping me edit Holy Miracles. And many thanks to my husband Edward for his love and support.

Introduction

I can remember as far back in my teens of having an instinctive feeling to write, although at the same time, wondering write about what? I didn't know then, that those feelings were coming from my intuition or might have been the angels communicating to me, to write of my spiritual experiences I was yet to encounter with God, Jesus Christ and the Heavenly Angels.

Now in my fifties as I reflect back at all my incredible experiences, I am astounded with the great love God and Jesus has for all of us, and the magnitude of God's power to create miracles. No miracle is too great or too small, from bringing me a cup of coffee, to creating snow so far down in the south.

These are my true, amazing miracles I wish to share with you.

Contents

Mother Mary by My Bed

In my early teens, I lived with my family in an eerie three-bedroom old house. One moonless dark night I woke up to a full bladder. I sat up in bed for a few minutes looking around the dark room and hallway. There were two bathrooms. One was in the long hallway which was farther away, and the other one was closer but next to a large scary closet. For some reason, I felt bad vibes coming from that closet. It gave me the creeps, especially at night. I contemplated which of the two was the least scary. Even though I had gone to the bathroom many times in the dark before, it was still frightening every time, plus I had the feeling of someone watching.

Suddenly, the Holy Mother Mary appeared before me at the foot end of the bed. I was astonished and wondered why she was there to see me. I thought to myself, "Who am I to deserve her visit?" All my fears vanished as I looked upon her. She was transparent but was outlined in beautiful vibrant colors of light throughout. The outline of her veil was a beautiful blue and her dress was outlined in white. She seemed to be carrying something, but at the time my eyes were focused on her, and I didn't notice what she was carrying. Then as I reached over to touch her, she disappeared.

I laid back in bed for a while to mull over what had just happened. I could not believe I saw Mother Mary with my own eyes. After going over the experience a few times in my head, I then ran to the bathroom by the scary closet and ran back to bed.

I felt protected and loved after seeing her that night.

Hand From Heaven Held My Car Back

B ack in the year of 1985 in Corpus Christi, the main freeway was still under construction. At the end of the completed freeway, began a one way, two-lane street. The other two-lane street went the opposite direction.

One sunny morning, I was driving my husband to work on the two-lane street. We were both running late, so I was speeding a little over the speed limit, when the traffic slowed me down. I was stuck behind a slow moving, beat up car. I was unable to pass due to the cars on my right, so I was forced to drive at a slow speed behind it. I could see the freeway up ahead and thought as soon as I get to the beginning of the freeway, I will quickly speed up and pass the slow moving car to the left.

The freeway was getting closer and I was getting ready to stomp on the gas peddle, but just as I approached the freeway, I saw a huge, black outline of a hand reaching down from the sky. It was right in front of my car, as if trying to

3

hold my car back. For some reason, it didn't want me to go forward. I was so fascinated with the hand, that instead of speeding up, I slowed down to watch it.

From the corner of my eye, I could see my husband who was sitting in the passenger side, staring at me, with the look of confusion, as to why I wasn't speeding up to pass the car.

Just as the hand disappears, the slow moving car in front of me has a blow out and drives off to the left side to get out of the way where I was heading to, if I had accelerated. I thought, "Unbelievable. If it wasn't for the hand that slowed me down, I would have had a bad accident."

Someone from heaven saved me from crashing that day.

The Dark Cloud

It was a clear sunny morning and I was driving on the cross town freeway on my way to work. As I glanced in the rear view mirror to see the traffic behind me, I was startled and in disbelief, as to what I saw. There was a large smoky black, dark cloud hovering above the cars behind me. It was moving at the same speed with the cars. It seemed as though the dark cloud was following the people that were in those cars. I could not believe what I was seeing. I looked forward for a second at the cars ahead of me and then looked back again in the rear-view mirror, but I no longer was able to see it.

The first thing that came to my mind was that it must have been the evil in this earth that is always following us around. The evil that is waiting around for opportunities to cause trouble in our lives, and I just happened to get a glimpse of it.

A few years passed after this incident and then on one Halloween night, my husband had heard that a group of people were going to be playing Halloween music at a Church and he wanted to go.

Upon arriving we were stunned to find that the group was performing the Halloween music inside the Church, instead of the other buildings which I assumed it would be. I said to my husband, "Isn't the Church supposed to be kept holy?" Even the people performing were wearing evil Halloween costumes inside the Church. I couldn't believe they were doing this. Didn't they know this wasn't right? I was upset with the whole thing.

That night I had a horrible, vivid dream. In the dream, I was in that same Church. I was sitting in one of the pews along with the other people who were there. Out of nowhere, a black cloud came in through the ceiling and into the Church. We all franticly ran out of the church. It was the same dark black cloud I had seen a few years back in my rear view mirror.

I've always know that evil is always lurking around us trying to cause havoc in our lives. It tries to manipulate our minds into doing bad things. I believe that dark cloud hovers over the people it can easily control into having evil thoughts, starting arguments, killing, stealing, hating, you name it.

Having God in our daily lives repels that evil dark cloud away from us.

My Elevator to Heaven

Having had many spiritual experiences in the past, I began to wonder maybe I can have a conversation with God. I have so many questions to ask him.

So, I began asking him in my prayers to have an actual conversation with me. Weeks went by and I continued asking every day and night.

Well one Sunday morning during the Church service at St. Peter's By the Sea, the pastor asked those that wished to go up to the altar to pray, to do so at that time. People were going up to the altar and kneeling to pray. I decided to go up there to pray and ask him again to have a conversation with me. I kneeled down, closed my eyes, and held my hands together to pray. It was a little difficult concentrating on my prayer, due to the noise in the Church. I could hear people's footsteps coming and going, and some of the children were either crying or talking out loud.

During my prayer, I again asked God if he would have a conversation with me. In that instant, everything went silent. The sounds of the congregation vanished. I didn't hear the children talking and crying, or the footsteps coming and going. Somehow, I wasn't hearing from my body's ears, but through my mind. I didn't feel my body or the touch of my hands which I held together in prayer. Then a door opened up from the top of my head. I saw a soft, white cord that was attached to my head, which seemed to be my elevator to heaven. Without any effort in my part, my soul swiftly left through my open door, went straight up into the sky and passed the clouds and beyond. All of a sudden I was somewhere in a quiet place.

Even though I couldn't see God, I could feel him listening and waiting for me to speak. Unfortunately, I didn't expect to be taken in that manner or in that instant and was overwhelmed with the experience, that I was speechless and could not think of the questions I had wanted to ask him. My mind was going a mile-a-minute and I was thinking, "Oh my goodness, I have God waiting for me to speak and I'm speechless." I was searching through my mind for the questions I had planned on asking him, but I just couldn't think straight. I could not believe this was happening.

It felt as if four hours had gone by, and I began to wonder what was going on with my body back at the Church. I began thinking, "Maybe they are trying to wake me up or waiting for me to get up from the altar, or just maybe the service was over and everyone left." All these things started going through my mind, and I didn't want to waste God's time anymore since I couldn't think of the questions to ask him, so I snapped myself out of it.

Suddenly, I was back at the Church still kneeling at the altar. I could hear the children crying and talking, and the people's footsteps coming and going. As I opened my eyes, I realized that I had only been gone for a few seconds, because people were still at the altar praying. I was a little shaken and as calmly as I could, stood up and walked back to my seat.

I felt a bit foolish and was disappointed at myself. I had God's full attention to have a conversation with him and I couldn't even ask him one question. I was dumbfounded in that I was able to reach him and have his full attention. I later apologized for bugging him and for wasting his time.

The Christmas Gift

I t was a week before Christmas in 1985, and my husband and I were out shopping for two extra Christmas gifts to give away for a boy and girl. We were at the toy aisle and I stood back to let him select the gifts. He grabs a nice truck for a boy, but wasn't sure which doll to get for a girl. As I watched him kneeling down to the bottom shelf, he was picking up different dolls to decide on. I was thinking to myself, "Well that's a nice gesture. My husband, a tall, muscular man, kneeling down to the bottom shelf looking for a doll for a little girl he doesn't even know." It was sweet. I wondered, "If heaven could see him now, they would be pleased." In my mind, I silently said to the Heavens, "I think he deserves to win a nice gift, like the lottery or something, after doing a good deed for the children."

God and the Angels must have been listening to me that day at the store, because three days before Christmas, the phone rang at nine in the morning. My husband answered the phone, "Hello?" The radio station's disc jockey replies,

"Congratulations! You have just won an Amana Microwave Oven!"

He was so excited! He had never in his life won anything before. Later that day he said to me, "That's funny. I was going to buy you a microwave for Christmas." That was a memorable Christmas and to this day we still have that microwave.

Jesus Christ Blessed My Little Girl

After the birth of my baby girl Samantha, I stayed home for two weeks straight taking care of her. Worried that my baby might breathe in germs if I took her out to run errands, I would get my husband to run the errands and do the shopping. I was getting anxious though, to go out and see the world again. My mother insisted I take my baby to church first and give thanks to God for my healthy baby girl, before taking her out. My husband and I agreed, and we decided to attend the Wednesday night service my mom attended at the Primera Iglesia Bautista.

The church wasn't crowded that night, so there were a lot of empty pews in front of us and throughout. My husband was sitting to my left, my mom to my right with my baby on her lap, and my nephew Michael to my mom's right. About halfway through the service, a middle aged man went up to the altar, and began singing the Lord's Prayer. His voice sounded angelic. He had a soft, deep voice that mesmerized me into a relaxed state. As I listened to him sing, my heart and mind focused on Jesus Christ and I told him, "Thank you for my little girl." It was then that I asked him to come see her and bless her. In that instant, I saw Jesus appear around four pews right in front of my mom who was holding my baby. He walked through the pews as if the pews weren't even there. He came and stood right in front of my baby. He was transparent, dressed in his robe and was outlined in a glowing, white outline throughout. I watched him as he looked upon my baby with a pleasing smile on his face. I had kept from blinking my eyes so I wouldn't miss anything, but my eyes were getting too dry that I was forced to blink. As soon as I blinked, he disappeared.

I glanced at my mom, my husband and my nephew to see their reaction, but no one saw him. They didn't notice anything. They just looked at me puzzled as to what I was looking at. No one saw him but me. I later wondered, "If no one else saw Jesus Christ standing there in front of us, there must be numerous times that he has stood by our side without us knowing."

Angel at the Pharmacy

While at the pharmacy to pickup my prescription, I noticed there was only one person filling the orders, and one person at the register. The person at the register was already helping a customer and I was the next and last one in line.

As I stood there looking straight ahead, I suddenly felt the presence of someone standing right next to me, although I didn't hear any foot steps. I thought, "Why is this person standing so close to me when there is so much room?" As I faced the pharmacist, I could see from the corner of my eye, the profile of a beautiful woman with long, wavy, blond hair, waiting patiently for her turn without saying a word. I noticed the male pharmacist didn't even acknowledge or look at this beautiful woman. I thought that was odd. I was beginning to wonder why? He never looked at her once or greeted her, the way he did with me when I approached the area.

Curious, I turned back pretending to look behind her

to get a look at her, but no one was there. She was gone and I didn't hear any footsteps leaving. She just appeared and disappeared. I realized it must have been my Guardian Angel.

Later that same night I remembered her. It was the same Angel in the dream I had back on May 5, 1994. I clearly remember the dream because it was a vivid dream and I wrote it down to remember the details.

In the dream, I was with my sister Alma in a car. She was driving and I was in the passenger side. We were driving down an unfamiliar street and we stopped at an intersection. We saw a woman walking across in front of us in the middle of the street. She walked quickly, but graciously. She had beautiful, long, blond, wavy hair which floated behind her in the wind. She was tall and wore a multi-colored, long, silky dress. I looked to my sister and said, "She looks like an Angel".

We stayed put at the intersection watching her and then she came walking to the driver's side window. The windows were open and she bent down to the window level and looked in at my sister and then looked straight at me. She said in a firmly but in a gentle tone, "Yes, I am an Angel." Her skin looked soft with an ivory glow and she had the brightest, most beautiful green eyes I had ever seen. I sensed that she wanted us to move along so we wouldn't keep her from her work here on earth. I felt a desire to go with her, but I knew we had to go our way.

The Angel at the pharmacy was the same beautiful Angel that appeared in my dream.

The Angel Baby Sitters

From the first day that my husband and I brought our baby Samantha home from the hospital, she has not slept through the night. Even to the age of four, she still kept me up for some reason or another. I was always sleep deprived and tired.

She was our only child and always wanted me there to play with her. I enjoyed every minute with her, but there were some days that I really needed a break to rest and sleep. Like the day of Wednesday, December 21, 1994, when the Angels stepped in to help me out.

That Tuesday night I was literately up all night due to insomnia. I had an early nine o'clock appointment, so I took my daughter to my mom's house and took off to the meeting. After the meeting, I went back to my mom's house to pick her up. By then it was eleven in the morning. My body was beginning to hurt all over and I began to feel drained due to my sleepless night. My mom was busy making tamales for Christmas and I noticed that she looked stressed. She had been having trouble with her back for a week now. She still had so much to do that I decided to help her even though all I wanted to do was go home and take a nap.

As soon as we were done making the tamales, I took my daughter home. I was exhausted. I remember thinking on my way home, "If Samantha would let me nap for one hour I would be okay." My husband was at work so it was just her and I that day.

We were home by one in the afternoon. I turned on the television in the living room and put her favorite cartoon tape on. I told her to watch cartoons while I take a nap and she said, "Okay." As I lay on the couch in the living room I said, "God, if I could just sleep for two hours, I will be able to keep going." I soon fell fast asleep and woke up at two. I saw Samantha playing with one of her games. I was surprised and I couldn't believe she was playing all by herself. She's never liked playing alone. I dosed off again and I awoke at three. By then she had put her games away and she was sitting at the dining table playing a different game. She saw me open my eyes and she came to me asking for a snack. I got up and gave her a snack and sat her up in her high chair in the dining room. Again, I went back to the couch and watched her as I lay resting and went back to sleep.

This time as I am waking up, I laid there with my eyes closed, listening to the sounds of the room. I could here the television and then I heard little foot steps running towards the couch where I was laying. I assumed it was Samantha. She jumped up on the couch right next to my head and she slapped her two little hands on my forehead. I felt the sting of her slap on my forehead and felt the couch sink down where she jumped. I looked up and said, "Samantha, be careful!" Only it wasn't Samantha. I saw that Samantha was still sitting up on her high chair watching television from the dining room. I didn't see anyone there on the couch with me.

I looked around the dining and living room from the couch and I could see these silhouettes from the waist up. There were around four silhouettes in the dining room standing across the table from Samantha and two or more in the living room, just standing around. It was amazing. I looked over at Samantha and thought, "Must be the Angels taking care of her."

I had a feeling they were all here to watch Samantha for me while I napped. It was four o'clock and everything was fine so I dosed off again. I finally got up at five, when Samantha came to me and said it was time to get up. My body didn't hurt anymore and I was feeling so much better. I couldn't believe the Angels came to baby sit my little girl so I could take a nap. Even the little Angels came. So amazing.

Out of Body Experience

It was nine o'clock at night on August 1994. My husband was working that night and my young daughter was sleeping in her room. I was laying on my stomach in bed for an hour reading a book about God and his Angels. My arms were getting tired of holding myself up, so I decided to lie on my back for a while. As I laid there, I could hear my heart beating. It began beating faster and faster. I could feel and see my chest pulsing up and down at a fast speed. I began to feel a fast vibration all around me. I looked over above me to my right and saw some small, white looking cloud-like figures floating above next to me which I understood to be Angels. I could feel their enormous love.

Then my spirit suddenly popped out of my body through my chest like a bubble. I no longer heard my heart beating. There was silence. There was no pain of any kind. The next thing I knew, I was somewhere else. I had left the human world and gone into the spirit world. I couldn't see anything since there was a soft, gray, thick fog all around me. I looked down at myself and I didn't have a body. Instead of having my physical body, I had a five-foot tall, fluid type, capsule shape body which had no legs or arms. I'm not sure if it was my soul that I was looking at or that I was covered in some type of heavenly blanket. It was a beautiful, navy blue rich color with lots of tiny sparkling stars all over. There was this feeling of peace and love all around me. There were no feelings of hatred, jealousy or envy like on earth. My life on earth seemed so far away as if I had lived it a long, long time ago. Time seemed to stand still and I wasn't sure how long I had been there.

I began to question, "Have I died?" I thought of my little girl who was home alone sleeping. She needed me and I couldn't leave her yet. Her unconditional love she had for me was the only attachment that kept me tied to life on Earth. I instantaneously found myself back in my body again. I felt sad for two weeks because I had wanted to stay, but eventually time erased my sadness.

Angel with a Sense of Humor

It was Mother's Day weekend, and my sisters and I had agreed to make a nice dinner for my mom on Saturday evening. Although, it had been a busy week and all I wanted to do was to relax and rest. I somehow ended up having to get all the groceries, plus cook the dinner since everyone arrived late.

Everything turned out nice and everyone enjoyed the dinner. Afterwards, everyone went outside in the backyard to relax and have a few beers. Not wanting to be in the hot, humid weather outside, I stayed inside to relax for a while in the coolness of the air conditioner.

As I sat relaxing at the dining table, I looked upon all the dirty dishes that needed to be washed. No one had initiated to wash the dishes and I knew my mom would end up doing the dishes. She always tells us, "No, leave them there. I'll do it later." I knew she would say that just to be nice, even though deep down she probably didn't want to have to wash them either. By then I was exhausted and didn't feel I had the strength to wash them. I got up anyway and began washing the dishes. As I stood there by the kitchen sink washing the dishes, I thought of just leaving everything and going home to rest. As I said that though, someone tapped my shoulder length hair which made my hair swing up into the air. I said, "Okay, who did that?" I turned around to look, but no one was there. Everybody was still outside.

I realized that it must have been my Guardian Angel with a sense of humor.

One time while at the bookstore, a book flew off the top shelf and landed on the floor with a loud bang which made me laugh.

On two separate occasions, as I sat at the edge of the couch watching television in the living room, I heard a tap coming from the artificial fichus tree which stands next to the couch. I look over to the tree where I heard the tap and I see one leaf moving back and forth.

Another time at the grocery store while standing by the can goods, out of nowhere, a can flew off the shelf and fell to the floor right next to me with a loud bang. Again, it made me laugh and I knew who did it. I picked it up and put it back on the shelf and continued my shopping.

Again, this time I was in the middle of the cosmetic aisle. I sensed someone watching me from the next aisle. Even though I couldn't see behind the aisle, I felt watched. I had my eyes set looking at the end of the aisle waiting to see who was coming. Then I saw a man walking from the next aisle and into the aisle I am in. I noticed that as he came into view, he already had his eyes on me as if he could see right through the aisle. He kept staring into my eyes with a smile as he walked closer to me. He had curly dark hair and brown eyes. He wore a white fishing hat with hooks, white casual dress shorts, white shirt, white knee socks and white tennis shoes.

His clothing somehow seemed off and funny. I tried to contain my laughter, but he knew I was laughing at him and he didn't seem to care, he just continued to smiling and looking into my eyes. He never took his eyes off me the whole time as he came down the aisle towards me. He came and stood before me, and he asked me of all things, "Do you know where the lipsticks are?" I was surprised as to why he would ask for lipsticks. He didn't have any makeup on and if he were married, I didn't think his wife would ask him to buy her a lipstick. I pointed behind me to where the lipsticks were without taking my eyes off his. He said, "Oh, thank you." He walked right past the lipsticks and out of my view to the next aisle. I thought it was odd, so I went to follow him, but I couldn't find him.

Well that day at my mom's house, after the Angel tapped my hair, I felt energized. I had the energy to wash all the dishes all by myself and then I went home.

Jesus Christ Walking on the Dry Grass

We were in the midst of a drought summer. The grass was extremely dry and I could hear the crunch, crunch, crunch, as I walked on the crispy grass. Even the leafs of the trees were shriveled up.

Two weeks after beginning a telephone marketing position, I realized it wasn't for me. I contemplated quitting the next day so I wouldn't waste my time, or giving it a few months to prevent hurt feelings.

The next morning I arrived to work early in the morning. I parked my car in the small parking lot and sat there for a moment contemplating my decision. In the distance I could see the rising bright, beautiful sun on the horizon through the windshield of my car. Next to the parking lot is a large, empty field of dry grass. I opened my car door and stepped out of the car. As I bent down to grab my purse from the seat, I heard the sound crunch, crunch, crunch, as if someone was walking on the crispy dry grass. I wondered who would be walking on the empty field this early in the morning. I heard the crunch sounds getting closer and closer towards my direction. I looked up to see who it was, but I didn't see anyone.

Even though my eyes weren't seeing anybody walking on the field, my ears kept hearing the crunching sound which was getting closer and closer to me. I was overwhelming surprised to see the translucent shadow of Jesus Christ walking towards me as he walked in front of the light of the bright rising sun. I saw his recognizable shape of his long hair and long sleeve robe. I watched in amazement as he walked in front of the rising sun, with the sun rays shining behind him. It was a beautiful sight to see. Once he walked past the sun I lost sight of him and the crunching sounds stopped. I knew he was still there next to me, even though I couldn't see him or hear him.

I understood he was there for me, to help me with my decision. At that moment, I knew what I had to do. That morning I told my boss that the job wasn't for me. He took it very well and confided in me that he was moving on too.

Angel Rescued Me from the Fall

One day during work, I had gone to the ladies room. As I came out of the bathroom stall, my high heel shoes slipped on the hard tiled, waxy, slippery floor. As I was falling though, I noticed I was going down in slow motion. Thoughts went through my mind, what if I fall and hurt my back and can't get up? I'll be stuck here for awhile. I said, "Oh my God, I'm going to crack my skull, please help." I tried holding on to the sink but I couldn't get a grip.

I heard a loud thump as I hit the floor, but I didn't land on the floor though. I must have stopped a few inches from the floor. Something or someone was there below me that cushioned my fall, because I didn't feel any pain. That loud thump I heard was from something else. After hearing the thump, I noticed I was a few inches from the floor. From there, I hit the floor. I walked away from that fall without getting hurt for the exception of a little scrape on my ankle. My hips didn't hurt or anything. It must have been my

Guardian Angel that took the fall for me, because nothing hurt on my body. I got up and went back to work. I was grateful and thanked my Guardian Angel.

A month passed and I was at the mall. To my left I witnessed a woman fall right on her back on to the hard tile floor. Unfortunately, they had to call the ambulance and take her to the hospital due to a head injury. She wasn't able to get up. I thought back to my experience and knew that, if it wasn't for my Guardian Angel, I would have ended up in the hospital.

Archangel Michael's Blue Light

I had heard of true stories of other people seeing Archangel Michael's beautiful blue light, but I hadn't seen it myself until one night in 1992. That night as I put my daughter to bed, I laid down next to her for a little while before going to my bed. As I laid there, I was feeling a little down and worried about a project that I've been working on for many years. It was taking me too long to complete and needed a lot more of my time to complete it.

Suddenly, I see a beautiful blue round light appear right in front of me in the middle of the room. I watched in awe as the beautiful blue light expanded and filled the room and then it vanished. I knew it was Archangel Michael's way of telling me that everything would work out okay.

Years later in early 2008, my daughter was going out to the mall with her friends. After she left, I asked Archangel Michael to protect her and keep her safe. Well that week she told me that she had seen a beautiful large round blue light that appeared and then disappeared.

I thought Archangel Michael must have known she would tell me, and probably wanted me to know that he was watching over her. My daughter didn't know I had asked him to protect her.

An Orb Came in Through the Window

One night after I put my four-year old daughter to bed, I laid there with her for a little while before going to bed. The night light that sits on top of the dresser by the window illuminated the dark room.

As I glanced around the room, I happened to catch a glimpse of a small orb floating in through the closed window and into the room. It looked like a delicate soap bubble. It was transparent with a luminous pretty green round outline, and about the size of a small round citrus orange.

I kept still and watched as it traveled above the night light and faded into the dark. I didn't feel frightened by it. I assumed it was an Angel.

Saved From a Car Crash

It was early in the afternoon on a bright sunny day. I was driving my car to a client's office and I had a box full of paperwork and brochures on the front passenger seat.

I was stopped at a red light traffic intersection. As soon as the light turned green, I pressed on the gas pedal to go. Out of the corner of my right eye, I noticed a fast movement of a speeding van coming towards the busy intersection. There was no indication of the van slowing down as it got closer to the red light. I turn my head to look and saw an older couple in the van. The man driving was too busy arguing with his wife who was sitting on the passenger seat. Both of them were facing each other arguing and didn't notice they were about to pass a red light at a busy intersection. When I realized that he wasn't stopping, I slammed on my brakes, but I knew it was too late to stop my car in time. I had already picked up some speed and would not be able to stop in such a short distance.

I immediately said, "God help". In that instant,

everything went silent and everything was moving in slow motion around me. The van drove by in front of my car in slow motion. I couldn't tell if he barely missed hitting the front-end of my car, or if he went through the front-end of my car. I could have sworn the van went through the front-end of my car.

As soon as the van completely passed through, everything was back in regular motion again and the sounds of the traffic came back on. All my papers and brochures that were in the passenger seat were all scattered on the floor.

It was a miracle. I knew God or his Angels must have helped me, because there was no way I could have stopped in time. I knew if God hadn't helped me, the van would have crashed into my car.

Message of 911

It was a week before the 911 tragedy. I had just finished with a load of laundry and was busy folding up the clothes in my bedroom. While putting the folded clothes in the drawers, I suddenly felt a presence in the top corner ceiling of the bedroom. I turned to look, but I didn't see anything. Then the presence spoke to me in my mind and said, "Something bad is going to happen. Don't be afraid. This is something that has to happen." In my mind I said okay and the presence left.

Even though I was told not to be afraid, I began to worry that someone might break into our house with guns or something. I had no idea what to expect. I realized there was nothing I could. Whatever was going to happen was going to happen regardless. I did my best to go about my day the best I could. Days went by and I was still worried about it.

Then it happened on the morning of September 11, 2001. My husband came home that morning after getting off work and turned the television on right away. He told me a plane had crashed into the Twin Tower building.

I knew there and then, that's what the presence was warning me about. I was heartbroken as I watched how things unfolded that day.

2004 Christmas Eve Snow

T wo weeks before Christmas, my daughter and I were driving to the mall to get some Christmas shopping done. We were making conversation on the way and out of the blue, she said, "I wish it would snow for Christmas. Why don't we make some fake snow and put it in our yard." I laughed at the thought of fake snow and said, "Why not have the real thing? Let's just ask God for snow this Christmas." She said, "Okay." At that moment, I looked up to the sky and with all my heart, I asked God for a white Christmas, knowing it had been a warm winter and that it rarely snows in Corpus. Slim chance I thought, but I also knew God could do anything. We continued to the mall and went on with the rest of our day.

Then two weeks later I am attending the five o'clock Christmas Eve service with my mother and daughter at the First United Methodist Church. It was a beautiful service with large displays of beautiful red Poinsettia flowers and the choir singing to Christmas music.

After the service, as we were walking out of the building, there was some commotion ahead of us. We could see that people were excited about something. As we walked out the door, we saw that it was hailing hard. I had never seen so much hail. It was breathtaking. Everyone was excited and thrilled. Down here in Corpus Christi, we rarely get hail or snow, so it was a big deal to us. We get in our car and drive to my mom's house in the hail. When we arrived at the house, it started to snow. We were all so thrilled and couldn't believe our eyes. It was a miracle. The weather man reported snow for only Corpus Christi and the surrounding towns. Everyone said it was a Christmas miracle. God does control the weather.

Later my daughter and I both remembered that we had asked God for snow two weeks before. We thought, "Wow! God gave us snow for Christmas. He answered our prayer." We stayed up late that night playing in the snow. It was a Christmas we'll never forget.

The Musical Orb

Around nine at night I was sitting on my bed reading a book, when my teenage daughter Samantha comes in with her guitar, wanting to serenade me with her latest piece she learned at school. So I put my book down and watched as she positioned her guitar on her lap and began to play. I was amazed by how beautiful and peaceful the music sounded.

As I listened and watched her play, a large white orb appeared right next to her by the edge of the bed. It had a white, cloud-like appearance and was about the size of a large oval watermelon. She didn't see it since she was looking down at the guitar and her long hair kept it out of her view. I kept quiet and still as I watched it. It stayed put about a minute and then began floating slowly behind her until it was no longer in view.

Thinking it was gone I didn't mention it, because I didn't want to frighten her. I figured it must have been an Angel who just wanted to hear the beautiful music. Before finishing the piece though, she stopped and said, "Mom, I just saw a white light fly behind you." I said, "Oh is it gone?" She said, "Yeah, it flew out the window." I told her it must have been an Angel who just wanted to hear the beautiful music too.

You Still Live On

O ne of my sister's friends had passed away and some of my family members were attending the funeral. I had wanted to go, but another sister of mine and her husband were in town and were staying with us. Plus, it had been pouring rain all morning and I had my year old baby to take care of so I didn't get to go.

A few years passed and then one of my mom's friend passed away and she asked me to go with her to the funeral. I did. It happened to be at the same cemetery that my sister's friend was at.

After the funeral service was over, I told my mom that I wanted to go see where my sister's friend was buried at. So we drove to the area where she was at and we both got out of the truck to look for the grave, but she couldn't remember the exact location of her grave. We searched for a while, but we couldn't find it. Suddenly in my mind, I heard her familiar cheerful voice, "I'm here, Eva. I'm right here." At the time, I had my eyes at one grave, and somehow my eyes were turned to look at another, and there it was. Of course, the small temporary marker had her first, middle and last name. But my family and I only knew her by her middle name which she had preferred to be called by. That was the name we were looking for. I didn't know her first name and that's why we couldn't find it. I yelled out to my mom, "Here it is." She came over and we stood there for a few seconds, but then out of nowhere, two large black dogs came running into the cemetery from the street where we were at. We ran to the truck and waited a while for the dogs to leave. I had hoped to visit with her for a while, but I didn't want to take any chances with the dogs so we left.

She must have known I was going to visit her and came to help me find her grave.

Then after my sister, Blanca, passed away on April 14, 2002, I began reading books on how to communicate with those that have passed on. I already knew that after the body dies, the spirit of the person still lives on.

According to the books, you're suppose to relax, quiet your mind and think of the person you want to contact. Well one night around nine, I decided to take a bubble bath to relax my body and calm myself. I lit a candle and relaxed my body in the warm soapy water. After clearing my mind, I began to think of my sister. Time went by and nothing happened. The water was beginning to get cold, so I decided to get out. I drained the water and reached for my towel. I had the towel in front of me and was looking down at the time, but when I looked up, there she was. I was shocked to see her. My jaw dropped and I froze. There she was leaning against the sink counter looking at me with her big eyes and looking healthier than ever. She was biting her lip the way she always did. I didn't get to talk to her because the moment I blinked my eyes, she disappeared.

Gnome Walked in Through My Window

Years ago, I read a book about a man who once saw a gnome walk across his room while reading in his bedroom. Shocked, he called out to the gnome and it angrily looked back at him for calling him and kept walking. I began wondering if maybe those old tales of elves and fairies were real. There are a lot of books written about them. The stories must have come from somewhere.

Then it happened to me. It was around ten at night and I had just lied down to bed, while my husband watched television in the living room and my daughter was in her room down the hallway with the light on. So it wasn't completely dark in my room, with some of the light shining in to my room from my daughter's room. I had just laid down on my back, and to my surprise, I saw a gnome walk in through my bedroom window and walk across the room into the hallway. I couldn't believe my eyes. I realized he was just taking a shortcut through the house and heading out to the front yard. He wore light cream colored shorts that came to his knees and a vest. He was muscular and walked the same way the cartoon dwarfs walk. I didn't dare call out to him because I didn't want to get him angry.

A few years later I was at the bookstore and came across a book on how to communicate with the fairies. I read the book and decided to do as recommended in hopes of seeing them. After all, I had already seen a gnome.

That night I had a vivid dream, I was being introduced to a two feet tall, adorable elf. His hands were tiny and his nails were green and pointy. His clothing was green. He was happy to meet me and had a big smile on his face as I bent down to shake his tiny hand. His home was actually right underneath our house. His entrance door was through the bottom of our cement front porch. I went in somehow and saw a large group of elves inside. There were rows of small beds.

In another part of the dream, I find myself standing before a large, tall tree in the front yard. The tree was happy to meet me and it bent down to greet me. I shook its branch with my hand. It was magical.

Jesus Walking Down From Heaven on a Dirt Road

One night while nursing a bad cold I decided to sleep in the living room fold-out couch, in consideration of my husband.

Everyone was sleeping and so was I, but although my body was sleeping, my spirit was up and wide awake. I was standing next to the fold-out couch waiting for someone. As I stood in attention, I turned my head to look toward the kitchen that was to my right.

Suddenly, I saw a dirt road appear with grass on both sides. The road was descending down from heaven through the ceiling and into the kitchen. Even though the kitchen was in the next room ten feet away from where I stood, the road seemed to go far in the distance.

Surprisingly, I wasn't shocked when I saw Jesus Christ walking on that dirt road coming to see me. It was as though my soul already knew he was coming and I was there waiting for him.

I watched as he walked in the distance towards me and then from one second to the next, he was standing right in front of me, as if he went warp speed. He was wearing a white robe and his hair was long to his shoulders. He had beautiful brown eyes. I even noticed the little lines at the end of he's eyes. He stood right in front of me staring into my eyes without saying a word or making any facial expressions, as if he was communicating through his mind.

I felt ashamed as I looked into his piercing eyes, that I turned my head away. I felt as though I was not working hard enough on what I came here to do. I sensed that his visit was just a reminder of what I was to do here on Earth.

The Cup of Coffee

Through our third-eye, we are able to see pictures, video-like scenes of things happening on this earthly plane and the invisible spirit world. Everyone has this ability. Although some people have it completely shut while others have it wide open.

On numerous Sunday mornings, I invite God to come have a cup of coffee with me as I read the newspaper. I usually place his cup of hot coffee at the other end of the table. Of course, it's just a thoughtful gesture and I just throw it away once I'm done with my coffee. However, I like to acknowledge him when I can. He does so much for me, I figure why not offer him a cup of hot coffee every once in a while. You never know if he's there or not.

Well one night, I had gone to bed in the living room foldout couch. I usually sleep there when either my husband or I are sick with a bad cold, so we don't wake each other with our coughing.

After fixing the bed covers, I turned off the lights and

sat in bed looking around the living room and dining room windows. Suddenly, a vivid scene comes to my mind through my third eye. I was no longer seeing through the eyes of my body, but through my third-eye that sees the spirit world.

To my surprise, I see a man which I knew to be God on the right side of the bed bringing me a large mug of steaming hot coffee. His arms looked firm and strong. He had silky, shoulder-length, snow-white hair, and his skin was youthful. He wore a white robe with a gold rope tied around his waist. His big strong hand held a large mug filled with what I assumed to be coffee with a white mist rising and over-flowing from the mug. He was smiling at a little, Indian girl who was to the left side of my bed. She was smiling and full of joy that he was bringing me this mug of coffee. As I looked at the mug, I wondered how I was going to hold it, since it was a lot bigger than our usual mugs we have here on Earth.

I couldn't believe I was seeing this. I wanted to see this through my physical eyes so badly that I forced my eyes to open and as I did, they were gone. I was so disappointed that I did that because I didn't get to taste the warm drink and missed an opportunity to visit with him.

Even though his hair was white, which here on earth we see it as being old and frail, he looked strong, handsome and wise. Well, it is written in the Bible that God made mankind in his own image.

I didn't know the little Indian girl and I didn't understand the meaning of her being there.

The Little Nail at Church

On Easter Sunday of 2008, I walked into a packed Church service at the Lord of Life Lutheran Church. People were standing by the side and back walls of the Church. I walked to the back of the Church to see if I could find an empty chair, when a man comes and tells me that there were two empty chairs at the front. He walked me to the empty chairs and I thanked him. Before sitting down though, I noticed something on the chair. I picked it up and saw that it was a tiny brown nail. I sat there analyzing the little unusual nail. I've never seen this type of nail before. I questioned, "Why is there a nail on the chair?" Of all the chairs in the Church, it happened to be on the chair I came to sit on. I tossed the incident aside.

Later during the service, the choir began singing many different songs. One particular song caught my attention though. It was a song about the nails Jesus took for us. They repeatedly sang the verse, "Jesus took the nails for me." As I heard them singing the verse, I was flabbergasted as I held the nail in my hand. I wondered, "Is God or Jesus trying to tell me something? Is this just a coincidence or is this a message from Heaven?" I even thought it might be a joke as I looked around the congregation behind me, but no one was laughing.

I was shaken a bit as I sat there receiving this tremendous message. The message, that Jesus Christ took the nails and died on the cross for all of us.

I still have the little nail tucked away. I later found out that it is a carpet tack used to secure carpet. I also noticed that the office is the only area in the Church that has carpet.

Still, out of all the people in the packed Church, how is it, that the little nail finds its way on the chair that I was escorted too? And throughout the whole service, the two chairs next to me stayed empty.

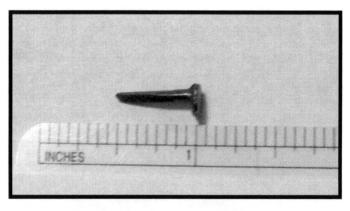

Photograph of the small nail I found on my chair at Church.

The Gift of Myrrh and Frankincense

Early Friday afternoon on December 21, 2012, my sister Ellie and I were Christmas shopping. After the last store we went to, I told her I was done with my shopping, but after saying that though, I remembered I had one more gift to get. This year, I wanted to get a gift for Jesus Christ. But what would be the perfect gift for the son of God? After some thought, I decided on myrrh and frankincense, just like the three wise men who came bearing gifts of myrrh and frankincense at the time of his birth.

So I bought a small pack of myrrh and frankincense and finally, my Christmas shopping was complete.

I arrived home around three in the afternoon and instead of wrapping the two little packages of myrrh and frankincense with Christmas wrapping paper, I placed it in a little crystal bowl on top of the shelf by the Christmas tree.

I did a few things around the house and then decided

to take a few photographs of the Christmas tree with all of the gifts underneath. As I looked at one of the photographs, though, I was surprised to see a large, beautiful white orb by the little crystal bowl of myrrh and frankincense. I knew in my heart it was Jesus Christ. I repeatedly took more photographs, but nothing else came out.

Then on Tuesday, December 25, at around two forty-five in the afternoon, I was picking up all the torn wrapping papers and boxes left on the living room floor from the gift exchange to take them out to the recycling bin. I walked into the garage and went outside where the bin was. I threw the papers and boxes into the bin and made my way back into the garage. I stopped to close and locked the door behind me and as I took a step, I heard a static sound and I froze. As I turned my head to look in the direction of the static, my jaw dropped as I realized it was the portable radio turning on, without anyone touching it. I heard the lyrics, "Merry Christmas, Merry Christmas." Then the radio turned off instantly. I said excitely, "W-o-w!"

I opened the door to the kitchen and yelled out to my husband that the radio turned on by itself. He explained that one of the buttons was a little loose, but that it had never turned on by itself before.

I have walked by that radio so many times before and it never turned on by its self. That was a special Christmas Day. I knew that was Jesus' special message to me.

This photograph was taken on December 21, 2012.
I believe it to be the spirit of Jesus Christ.

The Six Cents

I was just about done editing my manuscript for this book, when I read on the *Balboa Press* website, a division of *Hay House*, that they were having a contest for a publishing opportunity. I was excited about entering the contest in hopes they would publish it at no cost.

I enjoy reading many of the *Hay House* published books so it made sense to have them publish my book. Unfortunately, after reading the guidelines for the contest my manuscript didn't qualify because my manuscript wasn't close to the thirty thousand words required.

So my only option was to use one of their publishing packages and come up with the money to pay for it myself. But I didn't want to ask my husband about dipping into our joint account since I felt God and I should come up with the funds to pay for publishing the book since it was our project. Days went by and the thoughts of how to fund this project ran through my mind constantly every day.

Then late afternoon on Monday, March 11, 2013, I began

to have my doubts on getting the book published since I wasn't coming up with ideas to fund the book. I was inside the house and as I was slipping on my shoes to go outside and get the mail, I said to God, "Sorry God, I can't get the money. I can't do this. If you want this book published, you need to send me the money." I walked outside to the mail box and retrieved the mail without looking at the envelopes and walked back inside to the kitchen. I looked through the mail and there was an envelope from an organization with six cents inside. I thought, " I just asked God for money to fund the book and he sends me six cents, seriously?"

Bewildered, I took the coins out of the envelope and put them on the counter and threw away the letter and envelopes in the kitchen trash can. A few hours passed and the six cents were still on my mind. What can I do with six cents? Then it came to me. The coins were not meant to be spent, but are a clue or sign of where to get the funds. I remembered my collection of old coins which I have been meaning to sell, but never got around too. So I decided to organize them and sell them for cash.

Later that evening, I decided to keep the envelope that the coins came in, but was only able to salvage part of the return envelope from the trash can. Everything else was dirty and wet. The return envelope was addressed to *Food For The Poor, Inc.* and had a picture of a nickel and penny on the envelope. I later searched the organization's information on the internet and found that it's a large international relief agency. I thought, "Wow, God has his eyes on this amazing organization and the work they are doing." I know the envelopes were mailed to many households, but I feel there was a message in it for me from God in that mailing.

Then days later for my birthday, I received a generous check as a gift and the funds quickly added up to publish the book.

To top it off and this sent chills down my spine. On Sunday night, March 17th, I was reading my Pisces monthly horoscope from Susan Miller's *Astrology Zone.com,* and read that *"six heavenly bodies will align in Pisces early to mid-March"*. So not only did I receive the six cents on March 11, but six heavenly bodies were aligned in Pisces that same day. What a **coin**cidence! I felt that was a sign from the heavens.

Plus, those six cents also brought a message for us all. A message written by Robin Mahfood, President/CEO of Food For The Poor, *"I ask you to hold the enclosed coins in your hand, and know that you're actually holding a meal that could save a precious child."*

I don't think I will ever see coins the same way. As a teenager, I began collecting coins as a hobby. Now, coins symbolize meals that help feed the poor.

Here is some information given to me by the organization. As you can see, they do so much more than feed the poor. It's a remarkable organization.

Food For The Poor, named by *The Chronicle of Philanthropy* as the largest international relief and development organization in the nation, does much more than feed millions of the hungry poor in 17 countries of the Caribbean and Latin America. This interdenominational Christian ministry provides emergency relief assistance, clean water, medicines, educational materials, homes, support for orphans and the aged, skills training and micro-enterprise development assistance, with more than 95 percent of all donations going directly to programs that help the poor. For more information, please visit www.FoodForThePoor.org.

Orb Photographs

The following orb photographs are just a few of many that I have captured on camera. Some orbs are a solid bright white and some are transparent with an outline of half blue and half orange. One time I was about to snap a photograph, when I saw with my own physical eyes an orb on my camera's picture screen. It was the normal outline of half blue and half orange, but its outline turned completely orange as it zoomed out of my camera view.

One night, I quickly snapped a picture of the living room and found a lot of orbs in the picture. Some were on the couch as though they were sitting. Then I snapped a second picture just seconds later and nothing came out. They vanished. It's not the dust as some have claimed. Dust doesn't vanish on its own from one picture to the next.

To view a relaxing, 14 minute slideshow of my orb photographs, go to:

http://holymiracles037.com

This photograph captures a unique orb that I've never seen before. It seems as though the orb has wings. I enlarged the orb in the following photograph for a closer look.

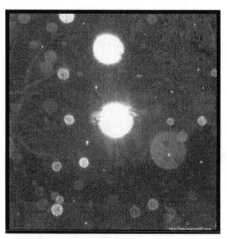

This is the close up view of the unusual orb from the above photograph. It looks as though it has wings.

Various types of orbs captured in the back yard.

Amazing large orbs.

Two orbs floating in our backyard.

I photographed this fast moving orb during a storm that was blowing in.

This photograph was taken during a storm.

Fascinating orbs with holes.

To view a relaxing, 14 minute slideshow
of my orb photographs, go to:

http://holymiracles037.com